Grow On

A Spiritual & Mental Wellness Devotional Journal

By April Y. Jones, LMFT

Published by Royalty Publishing

This book or parts thereof may not be reproduced in any form, stored in a retrieval system, or transmitted in any form by any means- electronic,

Mechanical, photocopy, recording, or otherwise – without prior written per- mission of the author, except as provided by United States of America copyright law

Unless otherwise noted, all Scripture quotations are taken from The Holy Bible, New King James Version, NKJV.

Copyright 2019 by April Y. Jones.

All Rights Reserved

978-1-7370485-9-6

Grow On

A Spiritual & Mental Wellness Devotional Journal

From the Author

PURPOSE

When I decided to write this book, I saw that there was a need for devotional resources that aim to target both an individual's spiritual and mental wellness. Through spirituality you can find and fulfill meaning and purpose for your life and through mental wellness, maintain a healthy psychological and emotional balance. I hope that during your navigation through this book, you will find helpful components that will tend to both your spiritual and mental wellness as you move forward on your growth journey. Please keep in mind that this book is not meant to be used as a substitute for a licensed mental health therapist.

PROCESS

As you work through this book each day, write down a self-affirmation and a bible scripture on a post it sticky note and stick it in a place where you can see it every day. Read the self-affirmations and the bible scriptures from the previous days and add to them each day.

Each day has a Challenge Yourself section. There is a journal page for you to write out your thoughts regarding the challenge and a prayer page for you to write a prayer specific for the current day's devotion. In the Challenge Yourself More section in the back of the book, you will find worksheets and activities to further develop your growth.

Please read the page about self-affirmations in the Challenge Yourself More section before beginning day one.

Day 1
Who Are You Becoming?

1 Timothy 4:15 (NKJV)

"Meditate on these things; give yourself entirely to them, that your progress may be evident to all."

As human beings, we are always evolving. The question to ask yourself is, "Who am I becoming, and who is it that I would like to become?" These questions may take some contemplation and a moment to meditate on. They may not even be questions you should answer swiftly, but instead, take extra care to put some thought into them. You know whose you are, but also knowing who you are is a prerequisite to knowing who you would like to become versus who you are becoming.

Who you desire to become and who you are becoming could have some differences. If you examine yourself and find that the person you are becoming does not look much like the person you desire to be, changes are necessary.

To bring forth these changes may not be an easy road to travel. Acknowledging some truths about yourself can trigger anxiety and other uncomfortable emotions, but still, owning openness toward your intrapersonal awareness is necessary for growth.

Also, exploring your connection and interactions with others—and the dynamics of those relationships—could give insight into how you may need to move some things around in your life. Although putting away things and people that stunt your growth can produce fear and other overwhelming emotions within itself, purging and creating space may be critical for your growth.

Sometimes, the process can become challenging, and you may want to justify a reason to stay the same—on the same undesired path—or look for a reason to discontinue the process of evolving into your desired self. It is okay to pause and sit with your thoughts and emotions for further, in-depth processing. However, stopping the process will only hinder becoming who you desire to become.

Cultivating and building upon those strengths already within you, and through prayerful guidance, positioning yourself to be used for your intended purpose are elements of bringing forth the person you are becoming.

Challenge Yourself

With change being an ongoing process, how do you feel about the personal changes you have made over the past year? Who are you now versus who you desire to become? Does the idea of who you desire to become align with God's purpose for your life? As you evolve, how are you being kind to yourself when the process becomes challenging?

Grow On and Journal
DAY 1

But also, Pray On
DAY 1

DAY 2
GROWTH

1 Corinthians 3:6 (NKJV)

"I planted, Apollos watered, but God gave the increase."

Growth transpires with effort. In order to grow, you must intentionally and purposefully tend to your whole system.

Think of a plant. A fully grown plant does not just appear out of nowhere—it begins as a seed. The seed must be planted for the roots to form. It must be watered, given sun, and taken care of for it to grow throughout the different cycles of its life. When it matures, it is strong, healthy, and fruitful. But if the plant is not getting what it needs, it will wither.

Regardless of where you are in life and the challenges you may be facing at this moment, you can sow the things into your life that will reproduce a holistically healthy person. When you sow those things into yourself, God will bring forth the beauty of the seed that you have planted.

Most times, it is great to have material wealth and financial gain, but most importantly, having spiritual and emotional maturity is essential to your overall growth and success as a being. While success is often measured by the strength of one's finances—and though it may bring fulfillment in some areas—it does not conclude the growth that is necessary for the entire system.

Growth produces good fruit that is determined by your purpose, values, behaviors, thought processes, and your spiritual and emotional intelligence. Growth enables you to act in your environment in a healthy way.

Learning yourself—what your triggers are, identifying false assumptions you hold on to, knowing your values, letting go of past hurts, and learning healthy ways of coping during challenges—can all be focal points of growth.

Challenge Yourself

In what areas do you desire to grow? What does your growth goal look like? What areas of your life do you already see positive change and growth? What current challenges do you face that may be a hindrance? Have you faced any obstacles or challenges that seemed to stand in the way of your growth goals in the past? If so, what were they, and how did you push past them to reach your goal?

Grow On and Journal
DAY 2

But also, Pray On
DAY 2

DAY 3
An Anxious Mind

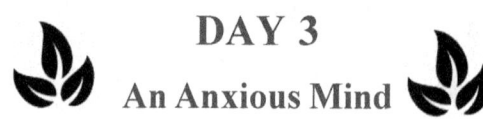

Philippians 4:6-7 (NKJV)

"Be anxious for nothing, but in everything by prayer and supplication, with thanksgiving, let your request be made known to God; and the peace of God, which surpasses all understanding, will guard your hearts and minds through Christ Jesus."

Anxiety can manifest physically and mentally in your body during stressful moments. The body's reaction to anxiety can differ depending on the person. When you become anxious, you may feel stomach discomfort, heart pounding, shakiness, you may sweat, or even experience dizziness. There is a plethora of physical symptoms that could occur due to anxiety.

Along with physical symptoms, the body can also react in other ways as defense mechanisms. These defense mechanisms are flight, fight, freeze, and faint. These are things that can happen to the body when you are confronted with a perceived threat. When you no longer feel threatened, the body can calm down, and these things will pass—then you will be back to feeling at peace.

Your spiritual and mental well-being could be largely impacted when your mind gets stuck in a constant cycle of anxiety-provoking thoughts. You can't seem to rest well, you're struggling with getting repetitive thoughts out of your head, and you are in constant rumination about an event, person, or thing.

If you find that anxiety tends to be one of those stumbling blocks that can get in the way of your growth goals, you may look into avenues to help you manage. Praying on these things and putting your trust and faith in God is one way to guard your heart and your mind from overwhelming anxiety and distorted thoughts. In addition, lifestyle changes, learning anxiety-reducing techniques, and seeing a licensed therapist may also be helpful.

Challenge Yourself

Meditating can help reduce anxiety. Take a few minutes when you pray each day to meditate. Take your thoughts deep and imagine leaving those things that ail and worry you with God, and taking with you pleasant thoughts and words of comfort. Try adding a very slow, deep breathing exercise into your moment of meditation while letting your body relax. Write down the things that seem to increase anxiety for you. What steps have you taken to work through it and bring yourself to a place of peacefulness? Also, write about your meditation experience.

Grow On and Journal
DAY 3

But also, Pray On
DAY 3

DAY 4
Thoughts

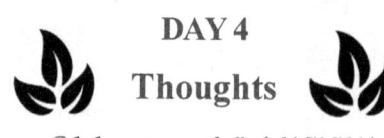

Philippians 4:8 (NKJV)

"Finally, Brethren, whatever things are true, whatever things are noble, whatever things are just, whatever things are pure, whatever things are of good report, if there is any virtue and if there is anything praiseworthy- mediate on these things."

Thoughts that are not true may enter your mind often, you are not alone. One's own thoughts can serve for their worst enemy. Especially when those thoughts are believed and constantly cycled in rumination through your mind.

Negative thought patterns can contribute to low self-esteem, depression, poor sleep, and other things that do not help you feel like the best version of yourself. Challenging those negative, untrue thoughts can help you replace them with true, positive thoughts.

Thoughts work together with feelings in a cycle. They affect the way you feel, and those feelings can be the force behind your actions. What a person thinks may not be the absolute truth; however, what a person feels is always real.

It's important to pay close attention to your thoughts and allow yourself to acknowledge them with compassion and non-judgment. It is equally important to acknowledge the feelings that come along with those thoughts and to be mindful of the actions driven by those feelings.

As you grow, your thoughts can become one of your strongest hindrances if you engage in a battle with them by trying to avoid or push them away instead of challenging them.

Challenge Yourself

One way to challenge unpleasant, irrational thoughts is to first acknowledge them. Write them down, and then beside each one, write a rational counter-statement.
For those negative beliefs that lean heavily on your self-esteem, practicing daily self-affirmations can help you create new beliefs about yourself and build your self-confidence. Continue writing positive self-affirmations and repeat them daily until you believe them, and the old negative beliefs no longer have power over how you feel.
If you have not already, refer to the self-affirmations page in the Challenge Yourself More section for guidance.
Use the journal space on the next page to write down how negative thoughts affect you now and how they have affected you in the past. Write about what you currently do—or have done—to help counter those negative thoughts.

Grow On and Journal
DAY 4

But also, Pray On
DAY 4

Day 5
The Spirit of Fear

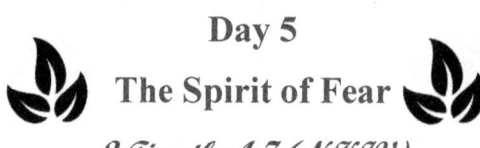

2 Timothy 1:7 (NKJV)

"For God has not given us a spirit of fear, but of power and of love and of a sound mind."

On Day 3, the topic was anxiety. Anxiety, at times, can stem from fear. Often, fear can be a stumbling block for moving forward toward visions, career goals, ministry, and other life goals.

When doubt settles into your mind, fear tends to follow closely behind.

According to scripture, to have a sound mind is not to be fearful. Most times, when doubt and fear set in, excuses are formulated as a defense mechanism—a way to settle the anxiety that fear has birthed into your spirit. You may begin to think things like:

"I'm not qualified for this."

"How am I even sure God called me for this."

"What if I fail at this."

"What will people think about me if I don't perform as expected?"

Do these questions sound familiar?

You may be wondering how you can move past those fear-provoking thoughts and into progression. You can practice challenging your thoughts. All the feelings and emotions that you feel are real, but not all the thoughts that enter your mind are reality.

To keep a sound mind is to rationalize and consider what is real—or what may be negative thoughts weighing in as a hindrance. Therefore, challenge those unwanted thoughts by countering them.

For example, if you are striving to progress into a new chapter in your life and that doubt-driven question, "What if I fail at this?" enters your thoughts, ask yourself instead, "What if I succeed?"

Challenge Yourself

When you are facing fear and doubt, write down those negative thoughts. For every negative thought, write a counter-statement for each one. Also, produce alternative solutions or "backup plans" if that will help you feel more secure about moving forward or diminishing fear.

This exercise can work for challenging fear-driven thoughts and self-doubt in all aspects of your life.

Journal about some of your fears and why you think you may have

Grow On and Journal

DAY 5

But also, Pray On
DAY 5

 # Day 6
Healing

Isaiah 53:5 (NKJV)

"But He was wounded for our transgressions, He was bruised for our iniquities; The chastisement for our peace was upon Him, And by his stripes we are healed."

When someone thinks about healing, they think about the body being sick with a physical disease and being made well. However, to be completely healed is to refer to the entire person. The entire person as a whole includes spiritual, mental, and emotional health.

To heal physical ailments, most people will go to see a doctor for a diagnosis, prognosis, and treatment, which is often followed up by prayer for their physical healing to prosper. Of course, it is important to manage and care for your physical health. However, mental and emotional health tend to get left behind—even in greater neglect than spiritual health.

Although mental and emotional health can be the most challenging part of healing yourself, mental and emotional healing—interconnected with spiritual and physical healing—creates a healthier person as a whole.

Spiritual growth is to learn whose you are and to connect to the God you belong to. To begin healing mentally and emotionally is to acknowledge the need to consistently evolve into understanding who you are as you change, to change negative core beliefs that may hinder you from becoming the best version of yourself, to develop emotional intelligence, and to reflect on behaviors that may be toxic to yourself and others.

Going to see a licensed therapist is one of the most productive ways to add to the nurturing and growth of your mental and emotional health. Many experiences throughout life—and traumatic events that may have left you broken—can be difficult to talk about or dig out of their hiding places.

Unburying those things with a professional mental health therapist can bring forth the healing that you desire.

Challenge Yourself

The process of healing may look different for everyone. From what do you need to heal? How have you begun healing spiritually, mentally, and emotionally? Has the process been challenging for you? Are you seeing a professional therapist? If not, why?

Grow On and Journal
DAY 6

But also, Pray On
DAY 6

 **Day 7
Forgiveness**

Ephesians 4:31-32 (NKJV)

"Let all bitterness, wrath, anger, clamor, and evil speaking be put away from you, with all malice. And be kind to one another, tenderhearted, forgiving one another, even as God in Christ forgave you."

A popular debate among many people is about what forgiveness looks like. Forgiveness can look different for each person. Some see forgiveness as accepting an apology and engaging in the same way they did before the offense. Others believe they can forgive someone and never speak to that person again—because forgiveness means releasing bitterness and anger but not necessarily rebuilding trust or reconnecting. It is important to understand forgiveness from a spiritual standpoint and examine your beliefs regarding what forgiveness truly means. You might agree that to forgive is also to be forgiven—and that bitterness and forgiveness are adversaries. To release bitterness, resentment, and anger is especially sacred for your mental and spiritual wellness. If these things are present in your heart, they will be a hindrance to your growth.

Therefore, forgiveness is much more for you than for the person who has offended you. Chances are, you have not truly forgiven if your emotions are still attached to the offense.

For example, if you still become angry about the money your friend never paid back last year, you have not released forgiveness into that matter—and you may need to have a conversation with your friend. Some ways to forgive hard situations are to pray and ask God to help you release the anger and bitterness you feel toward the person and the situation. You can also have a conversation with the person who offended you, which may help you gain an understanding that leads to forgiveness.

To be sure there isn't a deeper intrapersonal issue, examine yourself and explore the initial reason for the anger—and why it is so difficult to let go of the bitterness and resentment toward the situation.

As you work toward forgiveness, also be real with yourself.

Challenge Yourself

Growing up, what were you taught about forgiveness? What does forgiveness look like to you now? Do you find it difficult to forgive? What makes it easier for you to forgive? How do you feel when you have not forgiven someone? How does it feel when you have forgiven?

Grow On and Journal
DAY 7

But also, Pray On
DAY 7

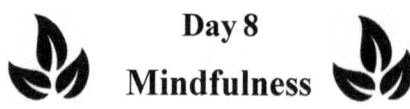

Day 8
Mindfulness

Matthew 6:34 (NKJV)

"Therefore, do not worry about tomorrow, for tomorrow will worry about its own things. Sufficient for the day is its own trouble.

Mindfulness is a practice used to bring balance and focus to the current moment while tuning into your thoughts and feelings. Mindfulness can become part of your daily routine if you consistently apply its techniques, as it is an ongoing practice.

Although meditation is one technique for mindfulness, mindfulness does not always require sitting in meditation. It may help decrease anxiety symptoms by bringing your mind from a place of worry and anxiousness about the future back to where you are in the present moment.

If you are like any other person on this earth, your mind has drifted off into tomorrow, next week, or further—while you were trying to enjoy your current moment.

Practicing how to bring your focus back to the moment by using all five of your senses to remain present is one form of mindfulness. You may be on the beach and begin to focus your attention on the way the breeze feels on your skin. You may tune into the sound of the waves as they crash forward toward the shore or notice the smell of the salt water. Maybe you'll focus on the shapes of the clouds in the sky as you lay back on your beach chair.

In doing this, you've brought yourself into the present moment—and maybe even out of a place of despair or anxiousness. Effective mindfulness practices are unique to each individual. Although it can be difficult to focus your thoughts solely on the current moment, the more you practice mindfulness, the easier it may become.

Challenge Yourself

Now that you have been introduced to mindfulness, can you think of a time when you may have practiced mindfulness to bring yourself to a place of peace?

Explore the components of mindfulness that may work for you. Try some of the mindfulness techniques provided in the back of the book, and journal about what those practices were like for you.

Did you find it difficult to focus? Which techniques were the most helpful? Which techniques will you practice as part of your everyday lifestyle?

Grow On and Journal
DAY 8

But also, Pray On
DAY 8

Day 9

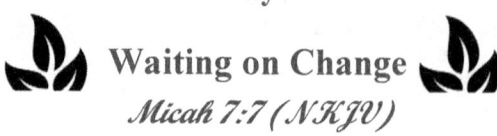

Waiting on Change
Micah 7:7 (NKJV)

"But as for me, I will look to the Lord; I will wait for the God of my salvation; my God will hear me."

If you often find yourself a little short on patience, you are not the only one. Waiting for a change while trying to remain in a state of contentment is tedious for many people—especially when that wait involves enduring longsuffering.

With patience being a fruit of the Spirit, and something much needed to sanely navigate many obstacles and seasons of life, the prayer to obtain more of it is common for many people.

Some seasons consist of waiting on change for an extended period. The good news is that just because you are waiting for your season to change does not mean you must be stuck in a mindset of despair.

God's "NOT YET" does not mean "NO," and His "NOT THIS" means there is something better in His will for you. God knows what you need and what you desire. He also knows what's best for you—sometimes beyond what you can see.

Waiting on your change to come means trusting that God is going to move you from your current position to the next level according to His will, by doing it His way.

If you find yourself struggling with your current situation—after you've prayed, applied the work required, and now you're at the point where all you can do is wait—you may find strength in seeking support from those around you whom you trust to give sound guidance and encouragement.

It's a blessing to have people who can pray with you and lift you up as you exercise patience through your waiting period. Being okay with reaching out for support in trying moments is not a sign of weakness; in fact, it shows strength.

Focusing on positive things and finding moments of gratitude may help you gain contentment while you wait for your change to come.

Challenge Yourself

Have you gone through a waiting period that was challenging for you? How did you exercise patience?

If you are currently in a waiting period, what might you do to help make your transition easier? What would it look like for you to be content during this waiting period? If you are experiencing—or have experienced—a significant amount of emotional or mental stress during a waiting period, have you sought a professional therapist? If so, what tools did you learn during your time with your therapist?

Grow On and Journal
DAY 9

But also, Pray On
DAY 9

Day 10

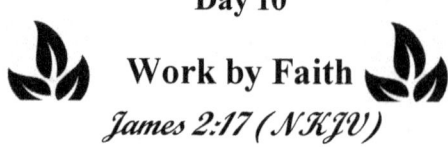

Work by Faith

James 2:17 (NKJV)

"Thus also faith by itself, if it does not have works is dead."

To know the depth of faith is to understand that it means believing something you hope for will happen—before seeing the results.

Being caught up in self-doubt can be self-sabotaging and may impede the progress of your desired outcome. A lack of faith can hinder your efforts. Internal struggles may convince you that you'll never reach the places in your journey that you long to be.

Faith and works are key components in manifesting the visions you wish to bring forth—including the fruits of your inner healing.

How you think about the steps you must take—and the work required to reach your goals, including those that focus on your spiritual and mental health—may produce fear and anxiety.

When fear presents itself at the door of your mind, if you allow it to impose on your thought process, it can diminish motivation and stunt the continuance of your growth, as fear is counter-conducive to faith.

Though you may not be able to see or feel the outcome, maintaining faith will produce the hope you need to continue working toward that which you wish to accomplish.

Believing in your healing when you feel so far away from it can be greatly challenging. However, faith can begin with just a thought. You only need a little bit of faith to start moving the obstacles of self-doubt and self-sabotage out of the way.

Understand that not all the growth you desire will come easily, but having the faith to produce the work required will yield positive outcomes. Believe that all things are working for your good according to the will of God.

Challenge Yourself

How has faith played a role in your growth journey? Do you find it challenging to maintain consistent faith as you work toward your growth goals?
Do you feel that you have faith but lack the initiative to work toward your growth goals? If a struggle with doubt has hindered your growth in the past, how did you overcome that doubt?

Grow On and Journal
DAY 10

But also, Pray On
DAY 10

Day 11
Peace

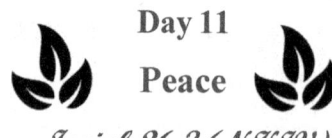

Isaiah 26:3 (NKJV)

"You will keep him in perfect peace, whose mind is stayed on You, because he trusts in You."

There will be challenges in life that you will have no control over. In fact, there's probably something you are facing in this present moment that you cannot change.

You may be seeking financial peace, peace in your home, peace at work, peace at church, or peace from uncomfortable thoughts. Whatever the situation, peace of mind is the goal.

Accepting that you cannot change every difficult thing that crosses the threshold of your life is essential to your peace of mind.

To be at peace is to dwell in a place of ease and calmness. Many situations and challenges can arise that disturb and disrupt your peace. Depending on how strong the brunt of those things is, it may be difficult to regain a sense of peace.

To be at peace is a scope of freedom that is essential for mental and spiritual wellness. Peace is a concept that can come to people in different ways.

The way in which you obtain peace may depend on the situation and the tools you possess to bring peace into your life. God says that when you keep your mind on Him, He will bring peace to you.

Instead of waiting for the situation to change in order to find solace, you can have peace of mind despite the circumstances—through prayer, meditating on the Word of God, caring for yourself, engaging in safe interactions and conversations with positive people you trust, speaking to your licensed therapist, repeating your self-affirmations, and using a plethora of other productive tools.

To create an ambience of serenity around you is to understand that you can maintain a peaceful mind in the midst of a noisy background by shifting your focus from the noise to the things that bring you joy.

Challenge Yourself

Do you find it difficult to have a peaceful mind during challenging moments? How do you seek peace during these times?

What would you say to a friend who is going through a challenging moment and struggling to find peace?

Situations sometimes happen that you cannot change—what can you do in those moments to create peace for yourself?

What have you done to create a space for positive energy to maintain peace of mind?

Grow On and Journal
DAY 11

But also, Pray On
DAY 11

DAY 12
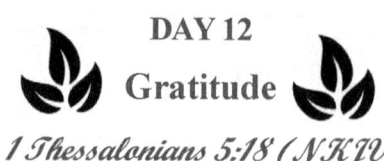
Gratitude

1 Thessalonians 5:18 (NKJV)

"In everything give thanks; for this is the will of God in Christ Jesus for you."

Gratitude, or thankfulness, is an essential practice for one's day-to-day happiness. If you're reading this journal, you've lived long enough to know that life can be unpredictable, and various seasons can bring unpleasant obstacles.

It is easy to get caught up and emotionally tied to those unpleasant circumstances, begin to feel defeated, and think that nothing ever goes right in your life. You might find yourself thinking that you have nothing to be thankful for when the things happening in your life seem contrary to what you are praying for.

You should be aware of what you are experiencing emotionally during these challenging moments. Be careful not to allow this kind of thinking to keep you in a negative place mentally. Be sure to practice gratitude amid those unpleasant circumstances.

Finding something to be thankful for may be a difficult task when it seems as though nothing is going the way you expected it to. It is not uncommon for some people to struggle with pulling the positive out of adversity.

Practicing gratitude may feel like a struggle, but it can come naturally once you make it a daily routine. Showing gratitude for even the smallest things can be a breath of fresh air. Something as simple as uttering thanks over a meal is a practice of gratitude.

Although it is the will of God for all beings to show gratitude toward Him, you can also practice showing gratitude toward the people around you. Whether it is your mate, your children, a stranger in the store, or yourself—the intentional gesture can be rewarding.

Challenge Yourself

A few common ways to practice gratitude are through prayer, meditation, and journaling. I challenge you to begin practicing gratitude daily through one of these practices—or whatever you've found works best for you.

If you choose, you can also keep a gratitude journal: a place to write down only the things you are thankful for. You can also practice gratitude by simply saying the things, situations, or people you are thankful for, while taking a deep breath and smiling at the thought of gratification. Journal about how it feels to practice gratitude. How easy or difficult is it for you? How has showing gratitude been beneficial to you?

Grow On and Journal
DAY 12

But also, Pray On
DAY 12

DAY 13
Wonderfully Made

Psalm 139:14 (NKJV)

"I praise You, for I am fearfully and wonderfully made; Marvelous are Your works, and that my soul knows very well."

Have you ever looked at yourself in the mirror and scanned the very details of your outer appearance? If so, how critical were you of your self-imagined flaws? Or were you able to look past what you may presume as flaws and see the image in which you were created?

People often look at themselves and think they do not have the perfect body, perfect eyes, or perfect face. But by whose definition of perfect are they setting the standard?

When you look in the mirror, you are looking at God's perfect, wonderfully made work of art. He made you just as He imagined and just as He wanted you—in the likeness of His own image.

I challenge you to look in the mirror and search yourself. Where you see imperfections through your eyes, can you accept them as God's wonderfully made perfections? What wonderful things can you find as you observe your outer temple?

I challenge you to look directly into those eyes that are staring back at you and say out loud, "God made me wonderfully."

Inner self-examination is just as—if not more—important than outer self-examination. You can clearly see with your own eyes who you are and what you look like on the outside, but what do you look like behind that outer person?

When God molded you, He didn't just mold your temple in the likeness of His wonderful and perfect image; He also intended for your inner spirit to be a match.

As you reflect, be kind and graceful toward yourself concerning what you recognize as imperfect. Your imperfections become perfections when God is invited to mold you on the inside. Allowing God to be the potter and giving Him access to mold you mentally and spiritually makes you wonderfully made.

Challenge Yourself

Explore your inner self. Who do you say that you are? Have you allowed God to mold your inner mind and spirit?

What characteristics do you own that have declared you "wonderfully made?" While there is always room for growth, what other characteristics do you desire from God to continue to perfect your inner self?

Grow On and Journal
DAY 13

But also, Pray On

DAY 13

DAY 14
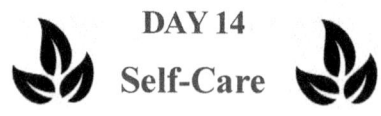
Self-Care

3 John 1:2 (NKJV)

Beloved, I pray that you may prosper in all things and be in health, just as your soul prospers.

Practices of self-care can be anything from getting massages, reading enjoyable books, talking to a friend, praying, and a plethora of other practices. One of the most important practices of self-care is taking care of your mental health.

Taking care of your mental health is equally as important as taking care of your physical health. Self-care is a form of self-love. When you take the time to love on yourself, you tend to feel better overall.

Taking care of your mind, body, and soul is a holistic approach to caring for your overall wellness. Self-care can consist of one or the other; however, a holistic approach to self-care may ensure that you find a beneficial balance for your whole self.

Becoming overwhelmed with day-to-day tasks and life's challenges can take a toll not only on your mental health but also on your spiritual and physical health. Some responsibilities in life come with taking care of others. Whether it is a child, a spouse, a parent, or maybe your career requires you to care for others to some degree, being intentional about the care you provide to yourself is essential to the quality of care you can offer those around you.

The popular saying, "You can't pour from an empty cup," is a piece of advice that speaks volumes of truth. You must refill, recharge, and find balance—or you will not possess the overflow required of you to pour out.

Whatever you do to provide adequate self-care in your daily routine, finding a regimen is ideal. It is important to find the techniques that work for you when establishing a self-care regimen.

Challenge Yourself

What does self-care mean to you? What self-care techniques do you use to recharge?

How do you pour into your whole being—mind, body, and soul? How is your self-care regimen beneficial to your overall health?

If you have found it difficult to create or stick to a self-care routine, or even if you struggle to provide adequate self-care for yourself, you may find the self-care worksheets in the back of this book helpful in assisting you with making those positive changes in your life.

Grow On and Journal

DAY 14

But also, Pray On
DAY 14

DAY 15
Self- Compassion

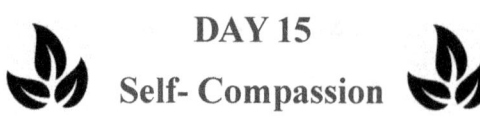

1 Peter 3:8 (NKJV)

"Finally, all of you be of one mind, having compassion for one another; love as brothers, be tenderhearted, be courteous."

Ahhh, the wonderful topic of self-compassion! Often, compassion comes much easier from one's soul when it's extended outward to someone else. To internalize that same self-compassion for oneself may be a struggle.

Most often, you may tend to be your hardest critic. Your own mind, sometimes, is your worst enemy. Self-compassion is to extend grace inwardly—putting away self-criticism and judgment, and forgiving yourself with love and tenderness.

Each person alive will find things about themselves that they may not like—flaws they wish they didn't carry and personality characteristics they wish to change. It is not a bad thing to acknowledge your own flaws, but how do you treat yourself regarding those things?

To have self-compassion is to have understanding and empathy toward yourself. You can make a mistake and still be a good person. You are allowed imperfections; even if you fail at something, you are still worthy. One of the most difficult areas in which people tend to find self-compassion is when it comes to their choices. The feelings of inadequacy concerning your life due to your choices may become overwhelming and may also become a repetition of ruminations.

Beating yourself up over a decision that did not yield its desired results will not turn back time. However, rendering yourself compassion—allowing yourself to make mistakes and to be okay with yourself if you fail—taking all the sourness with the sweet parts of you and turning it into tastefulness, is the antidote to moving forward toward desired outcomes.

When feeling inadequate, remind yourself that you are not the only one with these feelings. Some of the very same people to whom you extend compassion are the very same people who carry the same feelings and struggles that you do. Lend YOURSELF the same compassion that you give. You are also deserving of your own compassion.

Challenge Yourself

Can you think of a time or two when you easily extended compassion to someone? Can you think of a time when you struggled with lending compassion to yourself?
Why was it harder for you to have compassion for yourself than it was to show compassion to those people?
Think of a time when you were able to have self-compassion with ease. Why was it easier to show self-compassion on that occasion?

Grow On and Journal
DAY 15

But also, Pray On
DAY 15

Day 16
Speak Life

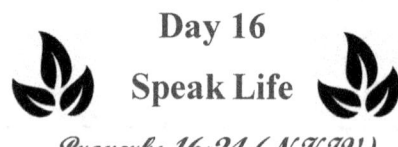

Proverbs 16:24 (NKJV)

"Pleasant words are like a honeycomb, Sweetness to the soul and health to the bones."

Choosing the words that you speak over your life should be done with care. Have you ever thought about the things you say that have become negative, repetitious statements over your life? One that is very popular is, "If it ain't one thing, it's another."

It is imperative to make sure that you are speaking the next best thing over your life, instead of the next worst thing—even when life appears to be pivoting out of control. Speaking life into what seems like a dead situation is exercising faith, and it can turn that situation around.

Speaking God's word over current situations—and those to come—without worry, can help decrease anxiety and depressive symptomatology. Speaking things as though you would like for them to be is to affirm your heart's desires and believe that your life will be graced with these things.

Self-doubt and negative talk have got to pack up and leave when they are replaced with sweet and pleasant words that comfort your soul. Learning to challenge unpleasant thoughts is a significant part of your growth. As you grow, exercising wisdom in speaking life over your situations is powerful.

Not only is it encouraging for yourself when you speak positive things over your own life, but it can be equally rewarding to encourage others as you do for yourself— to give hope to those who may need to hear it.

People going through challenging times often seek out those they know will offer an encouraging word—words of comfort and hope. They may not be inclined to confide in a negative Nate or Nancy, but are more likely to find comfort in someone who speaks life.

Challenge Yourself

What are some things that you have spoken over your life that have been manifested? How do you decide what to speak over your life?
Have you ever asked God to give you words to speak over your life and the lives of others? How do you decide who you will allow to speak into your life?

Grow On and Journal
DAY 16

But also, Pray On
DAY 16

Day 17
Loving YOU

Mark 12:31 (NKJV)

"And the second, like it, is this: You shall love your neighbor as yourself. There is no other commandment greater than these."

As easy as it may be to say, "Love yourself," putting it into action doesn't always come easy. Sometimes, loving yourself may feel more like a challenge—and it may even seem easier to love others than to love yourself.

However, how exactly are you loving others if you aren't LOVING YOU? Trying to love someone the same way you love yourself—while still needing to grow in self-love—may not reflect the kind of love God desires for us to extend outwardly. After all, you can only love someone to the capacity that you have learned how to love.

To be treated with love and respect is a healthy expectation. However, it is not realistic to expect someone to treat you better than you treat yourself.

How you LOVE YOU will reflect in the way you deal with those close to you and in how you treat yourself. You might find it hard to support friends as they excel, or you may envy the way they value themselves—because you desire that same kind of growth and long to value yourself in such a way.

You might talk to yourself in a way that reflects how you feel about yourself through negative self-talk. Maybe you do not feel that you deserve to be loved, so you are not very kind to yourself. You might allow others to treat you as though you are not worthy of the love you deserve.

Treating yourself with love requires you to extend self-compassion, to be self-forgiving, and to LOVE YOUR AUTHENTIC SELF while embracing your strengths and weaknesses.

Free yourself from the turmoil of comparing yourself to others. Examine your values and connect with your inner self on an intimate level. Knowing what you think, want, need, and feel can lead you to a place of self-love. To be aware of those things—and people—that do not respect your values, well-being, and peace reflects self-love when boundaries are set in place.

Challenge Yourself

How does self-care factor into self-love? How can you know that you love yourself? In what ways do you show self-love?

Why might it be difficult to love someone in a romantic relationship if you struggle with self-love? Do you believe you can love others sufficiently if you lack self-love? What do you think the love that God commanded us to show others looks like, when He commanded us to love others as we love ourselves?

Grow On and Journal
DAY 17

But also, Pray On
DAY 17

Day 18

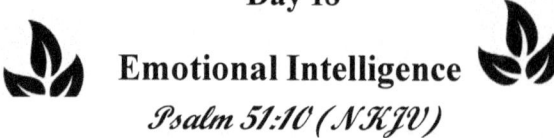

Emotional Intelligence

Psalm 51:10 (NKJV)

"Create in me a clean heart, O God, and renew a steadfast spirit within me."

To be an emotionally intelligent adult requires self-awareness, self-management, and the ability to identify with the emotions of others with empathy. The ability to maintain healthy and fulfilling relationships with your partner, your children, and others relies heavily on your emotional intelligence.

Being able to acknowledge your thoughts and emotions—while also being aware of the emotions of others—can help you navigate your interpersonal interactions wisely. Not only is becoming aware of your own emotional triggers key to advancing your emotional intelligence, but being able to manage them in a healthy way is essential as well.

Sitting with uncomfortable emotions may or may not be a challenge for you. As a child, many people learn how to deal with emotions. Some are taught that all emotions are okay, and those people may be in touch with their emotions. Others may be taught that all emotions are not okay and may tend to shut down instead of exploring their emotions—and may not empathize much toward others.

Depending on what you were taught about emotions, and how you saw others deal with emotions growing up could determine how comfortable you are as an adult with connecting with yourself and others on an emotional level. It is important to be able to sit with your emotions and allow yourself to feel them without judgment, as God designed us as emotional beings.

Being careful to take responsibility for your actions, acknowledging when you've hurt someone, and rendering an empathic, genuine apology when warranted is a display of emotional intelligence.

Additionally, spiritual wisdom can foster a growth spurt in your emotional intelligence. Knowing when and what to speak, how to react, and when to walk away can come from a place of spiritual maturity as well as emotional intelligence.

Being equipped with emotional intelligence can bring a wealth of peace to your life, even while managing situations within your societal elements. As you grow more emotionally intelligent, be careful to exercise self-compassion and forgive your imperfections along the way.

Challenge Yourself

What did you learn about emotions when you were a child? How have those experiences impacted your level of emotional intelligence as an adult?
How can you compare spiritual wisdom to emotional intelligence?

Grow On and Journal
DAY 18

But also, Pray On
DAY 18

Day 19 Relationship Goals

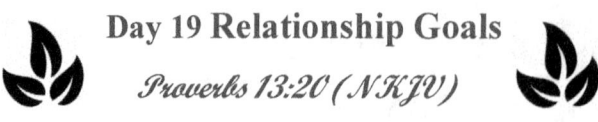

Proverbs 13:20 (NKJV)

"He who walks with wise men will be wise,
But the companion of fools will be destroyed"

Social interactions are one of the most important elements of being a human being. Most people thrive from interactions and connectivity with others. Who you connect with on an intimate level can have a huge impact on your growth and your mental and spiritual wellness.

There are several types of relationships that are important: friendships, romantic partnerships, family relationships, and—top priority—your relationship with God. All of these relationships have some form of intimate attachment when you are close-knit. In each of these categories of relationships, each person normally forms their own unique expectations or relationship goals.

Establishing your relationship with Christ first—and using your relationship with Him to guide you—can be the map for the rest of your relationships. When you know whose you are, you understand what you deserve and how you deserve to be treated by your partner, friends, and family members. Understand that you are a blessing, and you deserve to receive joy from your relationships—not pain and hurt. God intends for you to love others as you love yourself. This does not mean allowing others to walk over you, but rather assertively placing yourself in a position to receive love just as you give it. There are two things all healthy relationships have for certain: clear expectations and boundaries.

When building any type of relationship rooted in human connectedness, the ultimate relationship goal should be to be emotionally in touch with yourself, to clarify each person's expectations of one another, and to respect boundaries. Setting these things in place is the foundation of most healthy relationships. It creates balance and an understanding of your needs and the needs of the person with whom you share the relationship. If you find yourself connected to a person who does not respect boundaries, does not value you, or is not capable of reciprocity, you may need to evaluate the health of that relationship. Be aware of what the relationship feels like.

As you explore your relationship goals, it is important to remain self-aware of what you are also capable of contributing to the health of the relationship.

Challenge Yourself

What are your relationship goals for your relationship with God? What are your relationship goals for your friendships, family, and romantic relationships? What can you contribute to each relationship that can be beneficial to the growth of those relationships? How do you normally determine when a relationship is healthy?

Grow On and Journal
DAY 19

But also, Pray On
DAY 19

Day 20

 **Releasing Control**

Romans 8:28 (NKJV)

"And we know that all things work together for good to those who love God, to those who are the called according to His purpose."

To have control over the things that happen in your life will certainly put you at ease. Of course, there are some things that you do have the power to control—like how you choose to behave, what you choose to say, your likes and dislikes, etc.

Then there are those things that you have no control over. Challenges will arise when you relentlessly try to control things that you do not possess the power to change. Although difficult, it is in your best interest to liberate yourself from the urge to hold fast to that control.

Worrying about an outcome is the main reason for the urge to control. There are struggles that can come along with trying to control things that you ought to release.

You could experience anxiety on levels that affect your day-to-day social and occupational functioning. Stress could also result from relinquishing control, which may negatively impact your physical health, as well as your mental and spiritual well-being. The impulse to control can also affect your interactions with others. Trying to control situations—like other people's choices—could cause conflict and damage relationships.

Some circumstances occur as a result of a decision you made; some things are unforeseen circumstances of life. Either way, when you are faced with circumstances that you cannot control, the only thing left to do is to place those things in God's hands through prayer and release—then focus on what you can change.

Focusing on what you can change and what you can do in the interim, while having faith that God will work out the rest for your good, is more productive than focusing on what you cannot. You can continue in your growth as you learn to release control of the things you cannot change.

Challenge Yourself

Reflect on your life. Think about some personal things that you wish you could control but cannot. Then write about the things that you can change while you wait for God to work out the things that you cannot control.
How has holding on to the things that you cannot control affected you? What does it look like for you to release control of what you can't change and focus on what you can?

Grow On and Journal
DAY 20

But also, Pray On
DAY 20

Matthew 6:33 (NKJV)

"But seek ye first the kingdom of God and His righteousness, and all these things shall be added to you."

Challenge Yourself More

Self-Affirmations

Affirmations are thoughts that you think to affirm yourself—whether positive or negative. As previously covered in the Speak Life devotional section of this book, it is important to be mindful of the words you speak and the thoughts you believe about yourself. It is understood that some thoughts you may believe about yourself may have come from learned experiences and what you were taught about yourself as a child. Prayerfully, you begin to speak positive affirmations daily going forward.

Starting out, you may feel like some of the positive self-affirmations you are speaking to yourself are not true. This is because you already have some negative beliefs about yourself that are contrary to the positive affirmations you will create. Still, you must continue to speak positive affirmations. When speaking positive self-affirmations, you can bring those thoughts to life toward positive changes. Even the ones you start out not truly believing will overcome the false negative perceptions you carry about yourself.

As instructed in the From the Author section of this book, you will create your own positive self-affirmations daily. Prayerfully, long after you have worked through this book, those self-affirmations will remain a part of you and will project fruitfully and abundantly onto your life.

When you write your affirmations, you can write statements that reflect how you would like your life to be and what you would like to improve. These affirmations should be written in the present tense—as if to say, this is who I am now, or this is what I have in this present moment.

It is key that you say your affirmations with faith and that you replace negative self-talk with your positive self-affirmations. This is not to say that you will never have any negative self-talk. Remember that everyone is a work in progress. Have self-compassion, speak your positive self-affirmations with confidence, and GROW ON.

Some Examples of Positive Affirmations:

I am prosperous and abundantly blessed

I am sure of my ability to perform over and beyond in my career

I am a supportive and loving spouse

I have more than what I need financially

I am spiritually and mentally well

What's on Your Mind

It can be challenging to defuse anxious thoughts that just won't go away. Getting those thoughts out, instead of avoiding them may help to settle your mind. Use the spaces below to write down the anxious thoughts and then write a prayer specific to that thought. You can come back to this page whenever an anxious thought occurs that is difficult to get out of your mind to jot down more or create space in your journal.

Anxious Thought:

_____

_____

Prayer:

_____

_____

_____

_____

_____

Anxious Thought:

_____

_____

Prayer:

_____

_____

_____

_____

_____

Anxious Thought:

_____

_____

Prayer:

_____

_____

_____

_____

Anxious Thought:

_____

_____

Prayer:

_____

_____

_____

_____

Anxious Thought:

_____

_____

Prayer:

_____

_____

_____

Loving on Yourself

Self-love is an area that may require continuous growth and maintenance. It is easy to go about life and not really give much thought to everything that you love about yourself. Complete this activity to bring awareness to the wonderful things that you love about YOU and take note of how amazing YOU are. Then write a love letter to yourself on the next page.

What do you love about yourself?	What would you like to grow to love about yourself?

A Love Letter

Creating a Self-Care Plan

Being intentional about implementing self-care into your daily practices may require a mindset change, planning, and scheduling. When creating a self-care plan, be mindful that you can include small gestures of self-care throughout your day. Self-care does not consist solely of activities that take up a lot of time or require spending money.

Keep in mind, self-care is not just about going places or engaging in external activities—it is also about guarding your mind and weeding out negative thoughts, negative energies, and anything that adds stress to your life.

To ensure that you can prioritize self-care in your daily routine, you may need to incorporate things that take only 5 or 10 minutes throughout the day when time does not allow for more.

See a list below of some ideas you may use for self-care. Everyone is different and requires different things to reduce stress and remain balanced. Remember, you can do these things as part of a routine—not only when you feel stressed. Add your own self-care ideas to the list.

Get enough sleep
Create a relaxing bedtime routine
Eat healthy meals and snacks
Stretch or practice yoga
Exercise
Practice mindfulness daily
Visit the spa
Pray
Meditate
Go for a walk
Repeat self-affirmations
Read a devotional
Spend some time alone
Journal
Read a book that you enjoy
Watch a comedy
Spend time with loved ones who bring you joy
Have a stay-cation
Spend time outdoors and enjoy God's creations
Take a vacation
Keep a "feel good" folder and write down compliments you've received from others.
Avoid other people's drama

Place your device on DO NOT DISTURB
See a licensed therapist
Listen to music that makes you happy
Take a break from social media and the news
Dance
Try something new
Embrace doing things alone
Take slow deep breaths throughout your day
Sit in quiet
Light your favorite candle
Take a nap
Be kind to yourself
Have self-compassion
Forgive yourself
Do something nice for someone
Pray for others
Be mindful of your emotions
Treat yourself within your budget
Ask for help
Delegate responsibility when you feel overwhelmed
Take a day off to do nothing but rest
Say no when you need to
Get organized
Declutter your space
Talk to a positive friend
Create a healthy work/life balance
Find a new hobby
Take regular breaks when working on challenging things
Diffuse essential oils
Soak in the tub
Drink plenty of water
Connect with new people
Join a support group
Talk to a spiritual friend or family member
Read bible scriptures
Utilize your support systems

_____
_____
_____

Creating a Self-Care Plan (continued)

When choosing the things to help bring a healthy spiritual and mental balance into your life, it is important to be sure that your go-to choices are conducive to that goal. What you actually do and what you need may differ.

Think about the things you currently do, and evaluate whether those things are productive to your growth toward spiritual and mental wellness.

As you create your self-care plan, the questions below are there to guide you and to help you become intentional about sticking to your plan.

In the Challenge Yourself and Grow On section of the Self-Care devotional, you answered what self-care means to you.
Now that you have thought about what self-care means to you, what are your self-care goals?

What do you NEED in order to become happy, balanced, and at peace each day?

Are there any barriers that make it difficult to achieve your self-care goals or to implement what you need to reach those goals?
Think about what small steps you can take toward overcoming those barriers.

Make a self-care to do list. Implementing what you need. Think about what YOU CAN DO realistically on each day for the next week to make self-care a priority. Make a plan that includes at least one self-care desire for each day.

SELF-CARE TO DO LIST:

Sun
_____   _____
_____   _____

Mon
_____   _____
_____   _____

Tues
_____   _____
_____   _____

Wed
_____   _____
_____   _____

Thurs
_____   _____
_____   _____

Fri
_____   _____
_____   _____

Sat
_____   _____

It is easy to get caught up and busy with the things in your life and forget to take a moment to check in with yourself. Now that you have a self-care plan, program your device's calendar with your self-care to do list as a reminder to implement these things into your daily routine.
Keep it going. Be intentional.

If you are not at your best each day, or you've found it difficult to stick to your plan, it is OK. Remember to practice self-compassion by being kind to yourself.

Mindfulness

Practicing mindfulness can be refreshing and help you maintain a peaceful mind—even during challenging moments—because it can help you get out of your head and into the present moment.

Mindfulness, if practiced consistently, can become a part of your lifestyle and begin to come naturally as a healthy habit. There is a plethora of ways to practice mindfulness. I have listed a few below.

Try some of the mindfulness activities and practice them often to find what fits best for you.

Five Senses

During this activity, you will notice the things around you using all five of your senses.
Find something nearby that you can see and pay close attention to its details. What do you notice about it that you haven't before?
Listen for sounds and tune into the noises around you. What can you touch—or what is touching you? Be aware of how it feels against your skin.
What can you smell? Sometimes you may not be aware of the different scents around you, or you may pay them little attention. Take a moment to bring awareness to the smells in your environment.
Lastly, bring awareness to your sense of taste. You may notice an aftertaste from something you ate or drank earlier, or you may have a drink or some food present. Take a sip or a bite and bring your attention to what it tastes and feels like in your mouth.
You can practice this activity anywhere, at any time.

Being Mindful While Eating

Practicing mindfulness while you are eating is a way to take time away from everything that is going on and simply enjoy your food. Often, mealtimes can be rushed instead of relaxed.
If you are practicing mindful eating, focus only on your food and drink—nothing else. Bring awareness to how your food tastes, take your time, chew slowly, and be mindful of how it feels. The practice is about being okay with just being in the moment—present with yourself and your food—and taking your mind off other things. Take deep breaths throughout your meal and enjoy without interruptions.
If your mind wanders while you are practicing mindful eating, that's okay. Gently bring your attention back to the present moment and continue to relax.
Also, because food can be comforting, mindful eating can help bring awareness to emotional eating or eating simply out of boredom. Paying attention to yourself while you eat can reveal how you're feeling while eating certain things—and whether there's any guilt associated with what or how often you're eating, or if you're using food as a coping mechanism.

Mindfulness Breathing

Focusing on your breathing is another way to center yourself. The breathing technique you use matters.

As you take a deep breath in, your belly should push out—filling with air. As you slowly breathe out, your belly should deflate.

While you are breathing, be aware of how your chest rises and falls, and how your breath feels as it enters and leaves your body.

In doing this, you are focusing on your breathing, how it feels, the movement of your body, and you are attuned with yourself and your breathing in that moment.

You can take mindfulness a step further by bringing awareness to how your muscles feel in your body and whether you are tense or stressed. Your body reacts to what goes on in your mind.

Take deep breaths, relax your mind and your body. Practicing this daily for even one minute can make a meaningful difference in your overall mood.

Mindfulness Coloring

Purchasing an adult coloring book and using it as a mindfulness activity may be a great way to bring your mind to the present, as these books tend to require more focus than an average coloring book. Mindfulness coloring has been used to decrease anxiety. Focusing on the complex designs while tuning in to your creative side can be relaxing and may help bring you to a balanced place when your external world feels chaotic.

Set aside some time to practice mindfulness coloring using the attached coloring pages.

Relationships

Not only is it important to evaluate the dynamics of the relationships you have with those close to you—by being mindful of their values and the energy they bring into your space—but it is equally important to evaluate what you bring to your relationships, whether positive or negative, to ensure you are creating healthy interactions. The questions below are designed to help you reflect more deeply on your relationships.

What are your top three values?

Make a list of the MOST important people in your life.

Do you share the same values as those you keep close to you? If so, what values do you share?

What do you want to receive from the most important people in your life?

What parts of yourself do you give to those people?

Are any of the most important people in your life requiring more from you than you have to give?

Who do you desire to be in your most important relationships? Do those people give you space to operate as the person you desire to be?

Do you give space for the most important people in your life to operate as the person they desire to be?

What unhealthy patterns or behaviors have you noticed that you've presented in your close relationships and what work have you done on yourself to correct it?

What unhealthy patterns or behaviors have you noticed from others that is present in your close relationships and how have you handled it?

As you reflect on your most important relationships, what positive attributes do you notice from each of those relationships?

What do you need from yourself and how can you cater to your own needs?

Making a Change

Your work towards spiritual and mental wealth relies on your growth and growth requires change. Think about some positive changes that you desire to make that will increase your spiritual and mental prosperity. Work through the questions below as a guide.

Name the Change	Why
What change would you like to make?	List three reasons why you would like to make this change:
Level of Importance	**Actions**
On a scale from 1-10 with 10 being the most important, rate the importance of this change.	What steps will you take to make this change?
Support	**Vision**
Who can you trust to support you and hold you accountable during your change process?	What will your life look like once you make this change?

Personal Mission Statement

While you work on your growth you may want to create a motivational summary to remind you of your values, purpose, and desired outcome. Write your **personal** mission statement using the space below.

Other books by April Y. Jones

The Blended Family Series:
My Bonus Mommy
When Gigi Visits
Kiaria's Birthday Surprise

If it Makes You Happy

Set Me Free: A Journey Toward Self-Freedom- A memoir

On the Edge of Grace- A Novel

www.ingramcontent.com/pod-product-compliance
Lightning Source LLC
Chambersburg PA
CBHW081403070526
44583CB00020B/2653